FOUNDER'S NOTE

Ready to gain financial control and confidence?

Well, hello! My name is Octavia. I have a special place in my heart for the crazy ones - those who are willing to take chances and make bold moves to do what they love.

I began my entrepreneurial journey by taking on freelance copywriting clients while working a full-time job in advertising. Later, I started working on my passion project, Paper & Coin, while still primarily working for my freelance clients. Eventually, though, I was able to work on Paper & Coin full-time and build an amazing team around the brand.

At Paper & Coin, we're passionate about our mission of helping Millennials on all things money. Whether that's helping them ditch thousands of dollars of credit card and student loan debt, learn how to budget effectively, or how to start their own business; we're here for all of it! That's why we created this resource, just for you.

My team and I would love to hear about your entrepreneurial adventure. Share your story with us on Instagram or Twitter by tagging @paperandcoin. Let us know how this book helped you gain financial control and confidence while becoming your own boss.

Happy learning,

ORamirez

Octavia Ramirez
Founder/CEO
Paper & Coin

CONTENTS

03 Introduction

04 Side Hustles

13 Personal Finances

22 Business Finances

29 Taxes

38 Remote Work

INTRODUCTION

Build a Bigger and Better Business

Stepping out to "do your own thing" is perhaps one of the most difficult, yet most fulfilling ways to work and create a living. As a freelancer, you're an entrepreneur – the CEO of your own organization. That means, ultimately, the full responsibility of your business rests solely on your ability to make and manage your money effectively.

In this guide, you'll find simple, powerful insights, information, and inspiration to help you navigate and manage both your personal and freelance business finances. You'll learn how to gain financial control and confidence, and feel free to focus on bigger and better things for your business.

SIDE HUSTLES

Turning Your Side-Hustle into Your Main Hustle

If you're a freelancer, chances are you started your business as a side hustle ...

And, for many of you, your freelancing career is still a side hustle while you diligently work your 9-5 corporate job, or juggle between several different part-time gigs. Regardless of where you fall within that spectrum, it's all good - don't sleep on the process.

But, if you're like most ambitious Millennials out there, perhaps you dream of turning your beloved side hustle into your main hustle. To do your own thing - work on something you love and make a living while you're at it. This is absolutely possible, but it's going to take a lot of intentional steps, a thought-out plan, and a whole lotta chutzpah!

> " If you're like most ambitious millennials out there, perhaps you dream of turning your beloved side hustle into your main hustle.

4

SIDE HUSTLES

Is it a Hobby or a Side Hustle?

Chances are whatever you're doing, or thinking about doing, as a freelancer probably started off as a hobby. And, depending on where you see your life and career going, you may decide to keep certain activities as a hobby. But, if you decide to start capitalizing on your skill in, say, photography, candle making, fitness training, or basket weaving, there's nothing wrong with that. In fact, turning your hobby into a small business or side hustle can be one of the most exhilarating and fulfilling ways to make money, and eventually (hopefully) a living.

But, it's important to be honest with yourself here. Maybe you want to keep your hobby just for yourself as a way to unwind, relax, and recharge? Perhaps the added pressure of doing work for clients, or selling your work in the marketplace, may not make the task as enjoyable for you anymore. Turning your hobby into a side hustle doesn't necessarily make sense for everyone. But, for others, making money doing something you enjoy so much may seem like a no-brainer.

IT'S IMPORTANT TO BE HONEST WITH YOURSELF HERE. MAYBE YOU WANT TO KEEP YOUR HOBBY JUST FOR YOURSELF AS A WAY TO UNWIND, RELAX AND RECHARGE.

SIDE HUSTLES

Here are some questions to help guide you...

SIDE HUSTLES

When is the Right Time to Quit Your Job?

Ah, the age-old question that seems to plague almost every entrepreneur and freelancer - "when can I quit my job to pursue my business idea full-time?".

Well, my friend, the truth is, there is no right answer to this question. There's no one formula to follow that will make sense for everyone's unique circumstances. But, don't worry! We'll highlight some key things to keep in mind and help make things a little clearer as you navigate this decision for your own situation.

SIDE HUSTLES

WHAT QUALITATIVE AND QUANTITATIVE VALUE DOES/COULD YOUR PROJECT OFFER?

Depending on the product or service you're building, determining the value of that project may not be entirely clear.

Value is about so much more than just money or earning potential. And, although money is an important part of the equation, other factors of "value adds" of your hobby can help inform its revenue generating potential.

> **VALUE IS ABOUT SO MUCH MORE THAN JUST MONEY OR EARNING POTENTIAL.**

Say, for example, you run a blog all about organized living. You write weekly blog posts on everything from non-toxic, all-natural cleaning products, to the best closet organization hacks, and Spring cleaning tips.

Aside from the quantitative measures of value, such as web traffic, social media following, and email/newsletter subscribers, the inherent value of your blog is important as well. This qualitative measure is where a lot of the lasting value of your product comes from - how your work is affecting consumers. Are your readers trying out some of your organization tips? Are they sharing your content with their own friends and family on social media? Are they engaged with your content and excited for what you're putting out? All of this counts, and can have a very real effect on your bottom line, should you decide to start monetizing your work.

So, even if monetization of your hobby isn't clear or concrete at first, it's important to recognize the many other ways in which your work adds value to the consumers or collaborators. You can iron out your monetization strategy by then assigning a monetary value to those quantitative and qualitative value components.

There are several different determinants of the value of your blog, including variables like

01 MONTHLY READERSHIP AND TRAFFIC
02 SOCIAL MEDIA FOLLOWING
03 BLOG SUBSCRIBERS/E-MAIL LIST
04 ORGANIC, DIRECT & REFERRAL TRAFFIC
05 INHERENT VALUE

SIDE HUSTLES

HOW CAN I ADD FINANCIAL VALUE TO THIS PROJECT?

Using our example of the organization blog, start thinking about ways that we could leverage the variables of value we listed. What specific products and/or services could be associated with some of those things? In our example, physical products like storage containers, non-toxic cleaning products, or shelving units might be a good start. What companies sell or manufacture these items? Make a list of both those things, and then see how you could market, promote, or even sell them to your following on your blog. Many retailers now offer affiliate programs to influencers and vendors who promote their items online.

Or, you could have your blog or social media posts sponsored; this can usually be a faster, and more direct way of making money through your content.

And lastly, using our organization blog example, there may be an opportunity to even start your own line of all-natural cleaning products, or, creating and releasing an in-depth online course on organization and selling that to your audience? They are already fans and followers of your brand, and would likely be more inclined to buying a product or service that you've created since they know, like, and trust you from your blog.

As long as you think about the value you're offering, and how you can perhaps attach a price tag to some of those intangibles by creating products or services around it - the possibilities are limitless!

SIDE HUSTLES

CAN YOU WORK DURING FLEXIBLE HOURS?

As we talked about earlier, the nature of the business you're running, whether as a freelancer, solopreneur, or leading a small team, plays a big part in determining when you could or should leave a full-time job and pursue working for yourself full-time. If you're a freelance graphic designer, for example, you generally don't have to meet with clients every day, and quite often, are able to get briefed on a project, and even submit work entirely online. This type of business makes it very conducive to working another full-time job, and still continuing to build up your freelance clientele on the side. You could work evenings and weekends, and maintain frequent communication with clients. However, someone looking to start a daycare, for example, would most definitely need to run their business during traditional "working hours", and wouldn't likely be able to work another job at the same time.

ASK YOURSELF

What's the nature of your business? How flexible can your working hours be? How can you automate or digitize operations?

SIDE HUSTLES

HOW MUCH MONEY DO YOU NEED TO LIVE ON?

The next factor to consider is your personal living expenses. Tally up what your current living expenses are - everything from rent, car payments, student loan obligations, credit card balances, average grocery costs, and other essentials. If you were to "trim the fat" in your lifestyle, such as cutting down on eating out, luxury clothing, or entertainment, what's the minimum amount you'd need to make your basic living expenses and obligations? Now, does your current side hustle make at least that much after taxes? If so, then you're in a great place to consider quitting your full-time job and investing more time and energy into transitioning your side hustle into your main hustle.

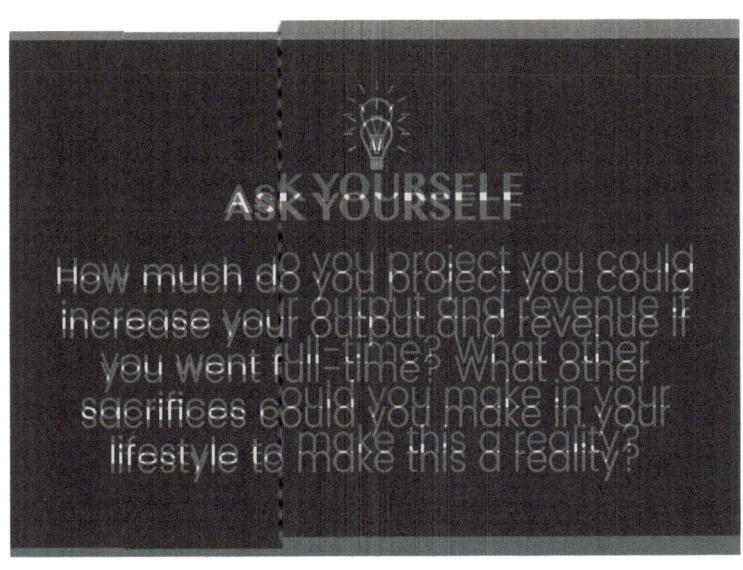

ASK YOURSELF

How much do you project you could increase your output and revenue if you went full-time? What other sacrifices could you make in your lifestyle to make this a reality?

SIDE HUSTLES

CAN YOU MAKE A 'SOFT PIVOT' INTO WORKING FOR YOURSELF FULL TIME?

When it comes to business, it's always best to remain fluid and agile - things don't need to be all or nothing. Consider ways that you could potentially decrease the amount of hours you work at a job, and start to ease into working on your business. This gives you plenty of time to build up your side hustle clientele, increase revenue, and not have the pressure of having all your eggs in one basket. Diversify your options when it comes to income. As your business increases, you can ease up on the hours at your job. Once you're able to project enough revenue from your business to match the income you need to live off, you can make the move into full-time freelance or entrepreneurship. But, until then, there's no harm in working both a full-time or part-time job, easing off your hours there, and simultaneously working within your freelance business.

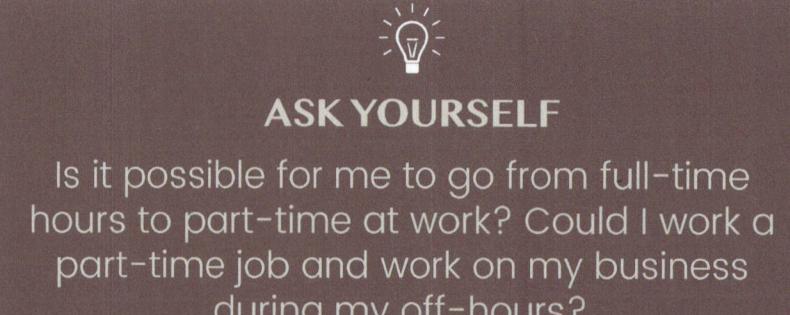

ASK YOURSELF

Is it possible for me to go from full-time hours to part-time at work? Could I work a part-time job and work on my business during my off-hours?

PERSONAL FINANCE

Can we get

... a little personal?

PERSONAL FINANCE

Get Your Financial House in Order

No matter how successful of a freelance business you build, unless your personal finances are in order, you'll never truly see how effective of a tool your income can be. You work so hard to build a business that you're proud of – one that affords you freedom and flexibility. It'd be a shame to do all that work, and not actually see the financial benefits that come with having a strong, stable personal financial plan.

In this section, you'll learn some of the key, non-negotiables of personal finance success. How you can take your income from your freelance or small business, maximize it, and make it work for your personal and professional life for years to come.

PERSONAL FINANCE

5 Non-Negotiables for Personal Financial Success

PERSONAL FINANCE

Like most things in life, personal financial success follows certain "laws of nature"

There are some best practices which, all things considered, have stood the test of time, and proven to help those that follow them gain financial control and confidence. The following principles are a slow simmer, no-nonsense, simplified approach to managing your money. They require focus, dedication, and intentionality, and when executed correctly, reduce the stress and worry that so many feel around the subject of money.

NOW GET ROLLING ON YOUR OWN DEBT SNOWBALL IN THE WORKSHEETS SECTION

01
Avoid every kind of debt...forever

Easier said than done, right? But, trust us when we tell you that getting into personal or business debt simply isn't worth incurring the risk. One the best ways to avoid debt is to avoid credit cards! In our years of coaching Millennials on personal finances, we've seen the crippling effect that high-interest credit card debt can have on people as they're already trying to keep up with living expenses, student loan payments, and sometimes dealing with unemployment and underemployment. Instead, try your best to live under your means with a budget (keep reading!), and cash-flow your expenses.

By avoiding taking on any form of loans, you're giving your income the margin and breathing room it needs to be able to pay off already incurred debt once and for all, start saving and investing for your future (including investing in your own freelancing business), and building long-term wealth.

PERSONAL FINANCE

PRO TIP

Got debt? We recommend using the 'Debt Snowball' method to pay it off. That's where you list all your debts in order from the smallest balance to the largest. Determine a certain amount of your income per month that you would put towards debt repayment.

Using that set amount, pay the minimum monthly payments on the larger debt balances, and put the remaining bulk of that money into the smallest balance debt. Once you've paid off that smallest debt, move on to the next largest debt, except now you're putting majority of the payment into that. Got it? Good!

PERSONAL FINANCE

02
Know where your money's going.

If we asked you what percentage of your take-home income you spent on take-out food, chances are you wouldn't be able to tell us. Look, we're not sticklers about tracking every dollar you spend. Although, that's definitely a great exercise to do for at least 1-2 months, just to see what your spending habits look like. But we are sticklers about having a budget and sticking to it. Tracking your spending for a little bit can help inform how much money to allocate in your different budget categories. Be realistic and set yourself up for success.

Download the Digital Budgeting Template at paperandcoin.ca/budgetingtemplate

03
Plan and stick to a monthly budget.

When it comes to creating a monthly (or weekly) budget, don't sweat the small stuff. Once you've taken care of the important things, like putting money into your debt repayment plan, or once you're debt-free, into your savings and investments, the rest is all gravy.

Having a budget isn't a restriction, and it isn't something that's relegated to broke people. You're going to need a budget throughout your life, regardless of how much money you make. In fact, the more money you have, the more you'll need a budget to keep things organized and on track. So, get used to this, and make it part of your financial lifestyle.

Get started building your budget with the BUILD YOUR OWN BUDGET page in the worksheets

If you prefer a digital budgeting solution, check out apps like EveryDollar or Mint. Or, if you're more old school, like us, use a good ol' fashioned spreadsheet on Excel or Google

HOW TO BUDGET ON AN IRREGULAR INCOME

01 Track your monthly expenses

For at least 1-3 months, see where your money tends to go, where you could possibly make some cuts. Do this by keeping receipts, checking bank statements, or tracking manually in a spreadsheet.

02 Plan from your lowest month

Use your lowest earning month as a reference for the least amount of money you would earn. What could you cover with your lowest earning monthly income?

03 Take care of essentials first

Your lowest earning month should be able to cover your basic expenses, including:
1. Rent/Mortgage
2. Groceries
3. Transportation
4. Basic clothing

04 Add supplementary expenses

Once your basic expenses are covered, you can begin to incorporate additional expenses, like bills and debt obligations over disposable spending. That means you'd cover utilities, student loan payments, and credit card balances before budgeting for eating out, buying new (unnecessary) clothes, hobbies, etc.

05 Have a 1-3 month "slack fund"

Depending on the nature of your business, you'll have both busy and slow seasons. During busier times, start saving up a fund to "pick up the slack" and hold you over during slower seasons. Having between 1-3 months of expenses set aside would be ideal.

PERSONAL FINANCE

04
Have a (proper) rainy day fund.
___

It may be a bright and sunny day today, but one day clouds will form and we may get a thunderstorm - that's why we own umbrellas, right? If that's the way nature works, then the same could happen in our financial lives. It's imperative that you have a financial umbrella, or a "rainy day fund" for moments when you lose a client, an expected deal doesn't go through, or an emergency hits.

Set aside between 3 to 6 months of expenses in a separate savings account. This money will give you the peace of mind you'll need when building up your freelance business, not worrying if you'll be able to make rent if business is ever slow. Or, if you lose a big client. You'll still be able to put food on the table.

PRO TIP

If you have debt, start by having at least a $500-$1000 emergency fund in a separate savings account. Preferably one that isn't directly connected to your day-to-day bank, so that you aren't tempted to use that money for anything other than an emergency. Once you've paid off all your debt, and now have less liabilities to worry about, you should work to beef up that initial, smaller emergency fund up to the standard 3 to 6 months of expenses.

PERSONAL FINANCE

05

Invest consistently for a long time.

Albert Einstein famously called compounding interest the 8th Wonder of the World. This is the principle that any money that you invest earns interest, and eventually you'll start earning interest on the interest.

> Here's an example, to make things super clear:
>
> Year 1: $100 + 5% = $105
> ($5 earned in interest)
>
> Year 2: $105 + 5% = $110.25
> ($5.25 in interest)
>
> Year 3: $110.25 + 5% = $115.76
> ($5.51 in interest)

If you invested $100 one year into a retirement account earning around 5% annualized interest, at the end of the year you'd have $105 in that account. That means your investment earned $5. However, the next year, you would earn 5% interest on $105, meaning you'll earn $5.25 in interest. Your interest is earning interest!

Now, imagine what that might look like if you invested $1000 a month in a well-balanced investment portfolio in a registered retirement account over 40 years? We crunched the numbers, and at 5% return, that'd equal a total of approximately $1.53 million in your nest egg. And, you'd have earned a total of approximately $1 million in interest! Not too shabby, right?

BUSINESS

It's Not Personal, It's Business.

As a freelancer or solopreneur, your business income and expenses are often so closely intertwined with your personal finances that you can't tell the difference between the two. Therein lies the problem. If you're going to operate a successful and sustainable freelance business, ya gotta keep your personal financial life out of the mix.

In this section, we'll talk about ensuring your business structure makes sense, how to systematize your business finances to stay organized throughout the year. And lastly, how to make sure you're prepared come tax season to pay the man; as little as possible, of course!

BUSINESS

What's the Structure of Your Business?

The legal structure of your business has financial implications that are critical to understanding how to manage your money in a tax-efficient way.

What is the structure of your freelance or small business?

SOLE PROPRIETOR

As a sole proprietor, you are able to operate your business under your own legal name, without having to register the company as a separate legal entity. That also means that your personal assets are liable to account for your business, should anything go wrong. This is the most common structure for freelancers and solopreneurs in Canada, and is often taxed at 40-45% of net revenue. However, just because the business is registered under your personal name, doesn't mean you should necessarily keep your business expenses coming out of your personal chequing account. We'll discuss this in more detail in the next section.

PARTNERSHIP

Similar to sole proprietors, partnerships have two or more proprietors who would be legally liable for the business. We highly recommend having written agreements between partners, accounting for how profits, workflow and responsibilities will be divided between all parties involved.

CORPORATION

An incorporated business is considered a completely separate legal entity, not tied to the owner's personal assets. They require a board of directors. They are audited far more frequently, and are often taxed at a much lower rate than sole proprietors, around 20-25% of their net revenue.

BUSINESS

How to Manage Business Revenue and Expenses

For most entrepreneurs, one of the most stress-inducing aspects of running a small business is managing the business finances. The problem is, we tend to overcomplicate this way more than it needs to be.

In this section, you'll learn the best practices for keeping your freelance or small business finances organized, simple, and worry-free.

BUSINESS

01
Avoid having a business credit card

First things first, just like in your personal finances, avoid any forms of debt in your business as well. That means not taking out any small business loans, and avoiding credit cards. Rather than using credit cards for business expenses, like buying supplies, paying vendors, or receiving invoice payments, use a debit card instead. This way, you're minimizing financial risk and liabilities, and it forces you to really plan and forecast your expenses ahead of time.

Create an annual and/or quarterly budget and plan for your business, and then, you're forced to stick to it as closely as possible. This might be challenging at first, but over time you'll get better at it. It'll help you hone in on your financial forecasting abilities, and also make you a pro at anticipating revenue and sales, and keeping expenses razor thin.

02
Have a separate business bank account

Next, where you keep your money has to remain organized in order for you to not lose your mind on this aspect of running your business. Most people end up merging their freelance business income into the same account as their regular pay cheque from their full-time job. And, while this is fine if you're running a side hustle with little to no expenses, as your business grows, so does its complexities.

For example, say you have an Etsy shop where you sell handmade quilts. As your customer base grows, you'll have to purchase more materials to meet the increased orders. Now, you have a steady influx of revenue streaming into your business account, as well as steadily increasing expenses, such as fabric, sewing needles, thread, etc. If left in your personal chequing account, keeping track of all this incoming and outgoing money could get messy, quickly.

Instead, set up a separate chequing account for your quilting business, and link it to your Etsy shop. That way, revenue goes directly into that account, and any expenses that need to be purchased can also come from that account.

BUSINESS

03
Use accounting software to track revenue and expenses

This brings us to our next step – just like your personal spending, it's important to track your business expenses. After you've set up a separate chequing account for your business, link that account to a cloud-based small business accounting software like FreshBooks, Intuit QuickBooks, or Wave Accounting. Trust us, rather than keeping track of your revenue and expenses manually, using these programs to categorize and track transactions will make running your business so much easier.

You can customize your expense categories within these software programs, and they'll automatically organize the transactions for you. And, they'll even provide you with monthly Profit and Loss (P & L) statements so you see how much is coming in and going out from your business account each month.

Once you've done this for a couple quarters or over a year, you'll have a better understanding of how much you're spending on different expense categories, and be better able to project and plan your spending for the next quarter or year. Over time, you'll have a solid grip on where to budget your hard-earned revenue year over year.

BUSINESS

04
Keep all your receipts

This might seem like a pain in the rear, but it's critical to keep receipts to justify your business expenses. This is especially important since you can't show chequing or credit card statements to justify those expenses. It has to be the original, itemized receipt of purchase.

By keeping your receipts and tracking your business expenses in an accounting software, you could lower your taxes by showing less profit. This is a great reason to re-invest back into your business, rather than paying more than you need to in taxes. And, if you're worried about hoarding little pieces of receipt paper, most accounting softwares now have receipt management or tracking apps, where you simply take a photo of the receipt and it'll categorize the expenses and log it into your business accounting software. Whichever way you choose to keep track of your expenses, just make sure you're doing so, and keeping proof of those expenses in case your business is audited.

REMEMBER

You must account for expenses over a 12-month fiscal year, that's twelve months from the time you started doing business. It is often accounted for between Jan. 1 to Dec. 31, or you can choose to pay quarterly, whatever you prefer. You only pay taxes on your net profits - that's the difference between how much revenue, or how much money your business made, minus the expenses, how much your business spent.

REVENUE - EXPENSES = PROFIT

BUSINESS

Give Me All the Deductions!

The Canada Revenue Agency (CRA) defines a deductible business expense as "any reasonable current expense you paid or will have to pay to earn business income". Depending on the nature of your business, a portion of the items in the list to the right can be claimed in your taxes.

A few things to remember:

1. Just because an expense is considered a write-off, doesn't mean it was free. Don't just go buying random things just to write them off to lower your expenses. Purchases should be made as investments into yourself as a business owner, or directly for your business. Keep operations and expenses as lean as possible.

2. If the item you're thinking of using as a business tax deduction isn't on the list, that doesn't mean it's not a legitimate business expense. Talk to a CPA about what could be included for your business

DEDUCTIONS

Rent
Mortgage
Interest
Heat
Electricity
Water
Insurance
Maintenance
Property Taxes
Cleaning supplies and services
Advertising
Cell phone or landline bill
Office supplies
Travel
Food & Entertainment (50%)
Conferences (70%)
Annual professional membership and license fees
Delivery, freight, and express fees
Gas and car maintenance
Legal and accounting service fee

Taxes

They say only two things in life are guaranteed - death and taxes. Now, let's make sure you don't drop dead when you see your business tax bill.

In this section, you'll learn the difference between your personal and business taxes, how to save up for each of them, and how to make sure you're not paying a dollar more than you need to.

TAXES

WHEN DO I NEED TO FILE TAXES BY?

Most individuals and businesses need to have their taxes filed in Canada by April 30. If you are self-employed, you have until June 15 to file without penalty. But any taxes owed will still be due by April 30.

In the early days of your small business, you may not have made a huge revenue or profit. Regardless, you still need to file the amount you made, even if it was a loss.

TAXES

WHAT DO I NEED TO HAVE TO FILE MY TAXES?

Firstly, when filing taxes, the structure of your business will determine the forms you'll need to have on hand for your tax accountant. Is your business a sole proprietorship? In this case you will file a T1 (personal) income tax return. For an incorporated company you will ask your accountant to prepare a T2 (corporate).

In addition to stating your income on Line 104 of your tax return, you'll also need to file Form T2125, called the "Statement of Business and Professional Activities"

For a T1 personal return, other common tax-related documents you'll need may be:

- T4 slips (if you have employment as well as business income)
- T4A commissions & self-employed
- T5013 Partnership Income
- T3 Income from Trusts
- T5 Investment Income
- RRSP contribution slips
- Charitable donations
- Medical and dental receipts
- Child care information

TAXES

HOW MUCH MONEY SHOULD I SET ASIDE FOR INCOME TAXES

Set aside approximately 30-40% of your gross revenue or income in a separate savings account. You'll be taxed on your net income; that's your gross revenue minus expenses (remember, we talked about why it's so important to keep your receipts and keep track of your expenses).

Unless you're working a regular full-time job in additional to having your side hustle or freelance business, your Canada Pension Plan (CPP) contributions are likely already taken care of through your employer. However, if you're self-employed, you'll have to pay for both your share and the "employer's" share. Thankfully, the employer half of the CPP payment can be tax deducted (i.e. subtracted from your income), while the other half will generate a tax credit for you.

If your business is incorporated, legally, it's a separate entity, meaning you'll need to complete and file its own Canadian income tax return. Therefore, you will also have to complete and file your own separate T1 personal income tax return.

TAXES

WHAT ABOUT SALES TAX?

At the risk of overwhelming you with Canadian sales tax law, let's keep things simple, and focus on the important stuff, shall we?

Almost every province except for Alberta and the territories - Yukon, Northwest Territories, and Nunavut, charge a provincial sales tax (PST) in addition to the federal tax, GST = 5%.

You are to charge HST (GST) to your customers on goods and services; you then have to pass (remit), or pay, those taxes that you collected back to the government. There is a small supplier exemption, where if your revenue is less than $30,000 per year, you aren't required to register for an HST number and collect that tax from your customers. You are, however, required to start charging and filing HST once you've registered for the HST number, even if you're making less than $30,000 a year.

Here's the total sales tax rate for each province:

Ontario - 13% (HST)

New Brunswick, Newfoundland. Nova Scotia, P.E.I - 15% (HST)

Manitoba - 13% (GST + RST)

British Columbia - 12% (GST + PST)

Saskatchewan - 11% (GST + PST)

Quebec - 15% (GST + QST) Quebec Sales Tax

Alberta, Yukon, Northwest Territories, and Nunavut - GST only, 5%

BOTTOM LINE:

DON'T BOTHER REGISTERING FOR THE HST UNLESS YOU'VE REACHED THAT $30,000 REVENUE THRESHOLD, AT WHICH POINT YOU HAVE TO START CHARGING HST.

TAXES

4 Simple Ways to Lower Your Tax Bill

TAXES

01
Keep a record of every business expense

As we talked about earlier, it's imperative that you keep a record of every business-related purchase you've made, including the HST you've paid on those products or services. The less you expense, the higher your tax bill will be.

Remember the formula :::
REVENUE - EXPENSES = PROFIT?

Well, in additional to saving taxes from deductions off the money you made, it also helps you save on the HST you owe the government.

HST paid - HST charged = HST owed

This means that the HST you paid on things like office supplies, graphic design contractors, or event venue fees will be deducted from the HST you charged your clients or customers on your own products or services. So, if you paid $2000 in HST on all your expenses over the year, but you charged a total of $4500 to your own clients, then the balance you have to remit, or pay back, to the government is $4500 - $2000 = $2500.

RECAP

You are only required to register for an HST number, and collect and remit those taxes if you're making at least $30,000 in annual revenue. However, again, if you register for an HST number before getting to that threshold, you have to charge HST.

TAXES

02
Invest money into an RRSP

Investing into a Registered Retirement Savings Plan (RRSP) is one of the smartest, and most efficient ways of not only lowering your personal income tax bill, but also saving up for the long-term. Two birds with one stone!

Imagine you were making $100,000 in revenue as a self-employed wedding photographer in Ontario. You're a sole proprietor, which means your business is tied to your personal entity. That means that outside of any business expenses like a new camera lens, or an assistant photographer or second shooter, the entirety of your revenue is reflected as personal income. If you invested $20,000 of that $100,000 income into an RRSP, you'd only be taxed at an annual gross income of $80,000. Basically, what you're doing is "sheltering" that $20,000 from taxes!

You can use the contributions you've saved in your RRSP to purchase your first home under the Home Buyer's Plan (HBP) (withdraw up to $25,000), or the Lifelong Learning Plan (LLP) (withdraw up to $20,000) to go back to school to upgrade your skills or knowledge as a mature student. However, even though you're allowed to take that money out for only those two programs, you have to pay back the money after 15 years for the HBP, and 10 years for the LLP.

You cannot withdraw any funds from your RRSP before retirement. If it's considered a way for you to shelter against income taxes, the opposite is true as well. Withdrawing that money for anything other than the HBP or LLP programs is considered an "added income" to your annual salary or business income, which means you'll be taxed on it, as well as charged up to 30% extra in penalty fees and withholding taxes!

We highly recommend you put money in your RRSP, and then DO NOT TOUCH until after your retirement party.

TAXES

03
Donate consistently to charitable organizations

Just like the RRSP, donating to registered Canadian charitable organizations is a great way to help out causes that you believe in and care about, while also saving on taxes! You can claim a non-refundable tax credit, up to 75% of your net income, including a full provincial tax credit, and up to 29% federal tax credit on donations over $200. You can even combine your charitable giving with your spouse to help further lower your taxes.

There are over 85,000 registered charities that are recognized by the Canada Revenue Agency (CRA), such as hospital foundations, religious organizations, or humanitarian aid agencies. They often see an influx of donations during the holiday season, and rely on that income to carry them throughout the whole year. We highly recommend committing to a few organizations and causes that you really care about, and donating consistently to help keep these organizations open, well-funded, and continuing to do great work in their communities, the country, and the world.

04
Hire a Personal Accountant

One of the best ways to save on taxes is to work with a professional. A Certified Personal Accountant (CPA) can help find deductions and credits that you're eligible for that you wouldn't have otherwise known about. They can highlight expenses you can write-off, and overall, help you keep everything organized and on-track.

The last thing you want to do is miss anything when it comes to taxes, especially ones that you owe. So, make sure to work with a trusted tax professional to put you at ease, and keep you and your business in good standing with the CRA

REMOTE WORK

What in the World to do with Foreign Income?

Is there any dream greater than being able to live and work on the beaches of Bali? Or, to blog from your favourite cafe in Paris? Or, perhaps shoot some amazing client campaigns in New York, Japan, or Berlin? Didn't think so!

Increasingly, Millennials are taking their talents across the border or overseas, living a dream that was once reserved only for prolific writers or painters – to do amazing work and live abroad.

In this section, you'll learn exactly how you can become a digital and creative nomad, working from anywhere in the world, while still managing your freelance finances and paying taxes appropriately.

REMOTE WORK

HOW DO I REPORT FOREIGN INCOME ON MY CANADIAN INCOME TAX?

According to the Canadian tax laws on foreign income, you treat foreign business income the same way you would handle business income from Canadian sources on your income tax return. That means, if you're a sole proprietor or part of a partnership, you'd report any and all foreign income as part of your business or professional income on Form T2125: Statement of Business or Professional Activities.

For example, if you're a freelance writer and blog for an American website, you would convert the payment you received in US Dollars (USD) into Canadian Dollars (CAD) at the time you were paid, using the Bank of Canada's exchange rate. Or, you can do this at a later date using the "average annual exchange rate". Once you know the CAD value of your income, set aside the taxes from that amount.

However, if you're actually performing your work in a foreign country, such as the United States, you may have to pay income tax in that country. Unlike Canada, the United States bases its income tax system on citizenship as well as where the work is performed. Canada bases its income tax system on residency. To further complicate matters, some states have state income tax and some don't. So, be sure to look into the specifics of the state you're working in, if you're living and working in the US.

REMOTE WORK

AM I STILL CONSIDERED A CANADIAN RESIDENT IF I LIVE AND WORK ABROAD?

If you earn all or part of your foreign income from working abroad you still have to file a Canadian tax return as long as you are deemed a resident of Canada. According to the CRA, you're generally considered a Canadian resident if you maintain "significant residential ties with Canada", including:

- Owning a home in Canada
- Having a spouse or children in Canada
- Having personal property in Canada such as vehicles, furniture, etc.
- Having health insurance in a Canadian province or territory
- Having Canadian bank accounts, credit cards, investment accounts, etc.

If many of the above criteria apply to you, you must file a Canadian tax return and report all domestic and foreign income in your tax filing. Also, to avoid being double-taxed, the income you earned abroad and paid taxes on in the country it was earned will be credited to you on your Canadian tax return! This is especially true for countries with which Canada has a tax treaty.

REMOTE WORK

For example, if you earned $30,000 of income while working in the United States and you filed a U.S. tax return paying $5000 in U.S. taxes, you would still report that $30,000 U.S. income on your Canadian tax return. But, since Canada and the U.S. have a tax treaty, you would be credited the $5000 you already paid the U.S. in taxes!

Canada has tax treaties with over 80 countries, including the United States, Mexico, UK, France, Germany, Italy and China. Some countries may require that you provide a Canadian Certificate of Residency in order to prove that you reside in Canada and are exempt from paying tax in their jurisdiction. You can apply for that certificate from the CRA. And lastly, if you're a non-resident, for Canadian tax purposes, you don't have to file a Canadian tax return.

You may have to pay additional tax on foreign income if the Canadian tax rate is higher. For example, if the Canadian tax rate on the $30,000 you earned in the U.S. was $7000, you would be credited the $5000 you paid to the U.S. in taxes, but you would still have to pay an extra $2000 in taxes to Canada.

REMOTE WORK

BOTTOM LINE

If you're a Canadian resident, as in you still call Canada your home base, and don't intend on losing that free health care anytime soon, then you'll continue filing a Canadian tax return by converting all foreign income into CAD. And, depending on the country you're living and working in, you might have to pay taxes there as well. But, if they're part of the 80 countries Canada has a tax treaty with, you'll be credited any of the taxes you paid to those countries. Just be sure to differentiate between your domestic and foreign income on the *T2125 Form – Statement of Business of Professional Activities*

42

REMOTE WORK

DO I CHARGE FOREIGN CLIENTS SALES TAX?

Don't charge international clients GST/HST.

You can still claim the GST/HST that you've paid for goods or services for your own business expenses, such as a new computer, printing business cards, conference tickets, that you purchased in Canada.

Also, when invoicing or charging international clients, make sure to keep exchange rates and transfer fees in mind when quoting them; that way you can rest assured that you're getting paid what your services are worth, and not losing money in taxes.

REMOTE WORK

Now, go live and work your dreams

Life is truly what you make of it. At the end of the day, the only person you're hurting with excuses is you. If you've wanted to pursue your dreams of starting your own small business, becoming a full-time freelancer, or taking a few months or years to live and work abroad, only you can make that happen! And, the great news is, you can do it! Don't short-change your life or your career - use the insights and tools from this book to guide you.

We love hearing stories of personal and professional success, and want to hear yours! Did you finally jump into that creative project you've been holding back on? Did you book that one-way ticket to Thailand to work as a remote graphic designer? Are you starting a yoga retreat company in India? Whatever your adventure is, share it with us by emailing **info@paperandcoin.ca** or tagging **#FreelanceFinanceGuide** and **@paperandcoin** on Instagram.

We can't wait to see all that you accomplish and put out into the world. Here's to you and your dreams coming to life, one financial step at a time...cheers!

DEBT SNOWBALL WORKSHEET

Get rolling on that debt snowball

$ _____

The total monthly amount you'll pay towards debt

DEBTS smallest to largest balance	MONTHLY PAYMENT minimum payments on larger balances	DUE DATE	REMAINING BALANCE

❗ REMEMBER

Once the minimum monthly payments for the larger balance debts are paid for the month, put the remaining bulk of your monthly debt repayment amount into the smallest balanced debt. Work your way down through all the debts until you're debt-free!

BUDGETING WORKSHEET

BUILD YOUR BUDGET

MONTH: _____

*This is a sample budget. Use this as a template to build your own based on your personal expenses, adding a new column to the far right for each pay cheque you get within the month. The two "total" numbers should be more or less close in value.

EXPENSE TYPE	EXPENSE CATEGORY	ITEM	AMOUNT	DUE DATE	PAY CHEQUE AMOUNT
					$ _____
FIXED	HOME	Mortgage/Rent Payment			
		Home/Renters' Insurance			
		Property Taxes			
	TRANSPORT	Car/Lease Payments			
		Car Insurance			
	MEMBERSHIPS	Gym			
		Netflix			
	UTILITIES	Cell Phone			
		Internet			
	DEBT REPAYMENT	Debt Repayment			
	SAVINGS	Travel			
		Retirement Investing			
VARIABLE	FOOD	Groceries			
		Eating Out			
	TRANSPORTATION	Car Gas			
		Car Maintenance			
	UTILITIES	Water			
		Electricity			
	MISCELLANEOUS	Bridal Shower Gift			
		Dog Grooming			
TOTAL			$		$

The Freelancer's Guide to Worry-Free Finances by Octavia Ramirez
Published by Kindle Direct Publishing for Paper and Coin Corp.

© 2019 Paper and Coin Corp. All rights reserved. Toronto, Ontario, Canada

The author of this book is not a professional account or financial advisor. The information provided within this book is for general informational and educational purposes only. No portion of this book may be reproduced in any form without permission from the publisher, except as permitted by Canadian copyright law. While we try to keep the information up-to-date and correct, there are no representations or warranties, express or implied, about the completeness, accuracy, reliability, suitability or availability with respect to the information, products, services, or related graphics contained in this Book for any purpose. Any use of this information is at your own risk.

For permissions contact:
Paper & Coin Corp.
info@paperandcoin.ca
Cover by Emma Johnson

Ready to level-up your financial game?

CHAT WITH ONE OF OUR FINANCIAL COACHES ABOUT HOW YOU CAN CREATE A STEP-BY-STEP **MONEY MASTER PLAN** FOR YOUR PERSONAL AND BUSINESS FINANCES.

Book your **FREE CONSULTATION** at
PaperandCoin.ca/FreeConsultation